What Does It Mean To Be Present?

By Rana DiOrio   Illustrated by Eliza Wheeler

Little Pickle Press

What does it mean to be present?

For Kara, whose talent, charisma, mettle, and presence inspire me.
— R.D.

For my family, who has believed in my abilities since day one.
— E.W.

Library of Congress Cataloging-in-Publication Data is available.
Library of Congress Control Number: 2010909660

ISBN 978-0-9840806-8-7

14 13 12 11   5 6 7 8 9 10

Printed in the United States of America

Little Pickle Press, Inc.
3701 Sacramento Street #494
San Francisco, CA 94118

Please visit us at www.littlepicklepress.com.

Does it mean showing up in class? No.

Does it mean sharing something at Show and Tell? No.

Does it mean wrapping yourself up? NO!

Being present means . . .

listening carefully when other people are speaking.

. . . noticing when someone needs help and
taking the time to give them the help they need.

. . . focusing on what's happening now,
    instead of thinking about what's next.

. . . appreciating what you have,
even if what someone else
has seems better.

. . . waiting patiently for your turn.

. . . treating each new experience as an opportunity

and understanding that making mistakes is how we learn and grow.

. . . being grateful for your
family and friends
and telling them so.

. . . savoring each bite of your delicious food.

. . . cuddling with your puppy and enjoying
how soft and wriggly he feels.

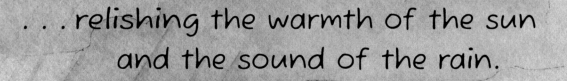

. . . relishing the warmth of the sun
and the sound of the rain.

. . . feeling the sand between your toes,
watching the rolling waves,
smelling the briny seaweed,

listening to the cawing seagulls,
and tasting the ocean's salty spray.

. . . allowing the rhythm of your breath . . .
in and out, in and out . . .
to make you feel peaceful.

. . . closing your eyes and being
still enough to hear your inner voice.

Being present means living in the moment.
It means realizing that . . .

yesterday is history,
tomorrow is a mystery,

and today is a gift—that's why we call it the present!

So tell your friends what it means to be present.

And spread the word—

when we're all present, life can be
much richer, fuller, and happier!

Our Mission

Little Pickle Press is dedicated to creating media
that fosters kindness in young people—
and doing so in a manner congruent with that mission.

Little Pickle Press
Media For A Better World

Little Pickle Press
Environmental Benefits Statement

This book is printed on New Leaf Reincarnation Matte, made with 60% postconsumer waste and manufactured with electricity that is offset with Green-e® certified renewable energy certificates.

Little Pickle Press saved the following resources by using Reincarnation Matte paper:

trees	energy	greenhouse gases	wastewater	solid waste
Post-consumer recovered fiber displaces wood fiber with savings translated as trees.	PCRF content displaces energy used to process equivalent virgin fiber.	Measured in CO_2 equivalents, PCRF content and Green Power reduce greenhouse gas emissions.	PCRF content eliminates wastewater needed to process equivalent virgin fiber.	PCRF content eliminates solid waste generated by producing an equivalent amount of virgin fiber through the pulp and paper manufacturing process.
44 trees	**20.0 mil BTUs**	**3,793 lbs**	**20,567 gal**	**1,377 lbs**

Calculations based on research by Environmental Defense Fund and other members of the Paper Task Force and applies to print quanities of 7,500 books.

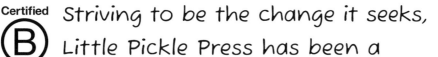

Striving to be the change it seeks, Little Pickle Press has been a Certified B Corporation since 2010.

About The Author

Rana DiOrio is skilled in the art of multi-tasking. In 1999, while sitting by the pool during a much-needed weekend away with a close friend, she was pecking away at her BlackBerry® when her friend turned to her and asked, "Does that device float?" Rana stopped working and started to enjoy the moment. It was about that time when Rana began to practice yoga, at first for exercise and soon thereafter for the peace and stillness it provided her mind. "It's so easy to get swept up in the swift pace of life," Rana explains. "I hope *What Does It Mean To Be Present?* conveys the importance of slowing down, being mindful, and savoring every moment."

Rana has written her way through life—as a student, a lawyer, an investment banker, a private equity investor, and now as an author and publisher of award-winning children's media. Her interests include practicing yoga, fitness training, reading non-fiction and children's books, dreaming, helping entrepreneurs to realize their dreams, effecting positive change in the world, and, of course, being global, green, present, safe, and kind. She lives in San Francisco, California with her Cowboy and three Little Pickles. Follow Rana DiOrio on Twitter @ranadiorio.

About The Illustrator

Eliza Wheeler was born into a family of musicians, artists, and teachers, and was raised in the north woods of Wisconsin. As a toddler, she adored crayons, and drawing has been her favorite creative outlet ever since. Eliza received her BFA in Graphic Design at the University of Wisconsin-Stout; shortly thereafter, she abandoned the mouse and embraced pen on paper to pursue a career in illustration. Now, Eliza has found her true calling — illustrating children's books. She has since written and illustrated the *New York Times* Bestseller, *Miss Maple's Seeds*, and illustrated the Newbery Honor book, *Doll Bones*.

While illustrating *What Does It Mean To Be Present?*, Eliza reflected upon her life experiences of being present: as a young girl, swimming in the Brule River and picking blueberries with her grandma; as a teen, running on long country roads; and today, hiking in the Hollywood Hills and walking to the farmers' market.

Eliza's interests include camping, reading, listening to music, and appreciating art. She and her husband live in Los Angeles "like two peas in a pod."

Other Award-Winning Books from Little Pickle Press

What Does It Mean To Be An Entrepreneur?
Written by Rana DiOrio and Emma Dryden Illustrated by Ken Min

What Does It Mean To Be Kind?
Written by Rana DiOrio Illustrated by Stéphane Jorisch

What Does It Mean To Be Safe?
Written by Rana DiOrio Illustrated by Sandra Salsbury

What Does It Mean To Be Green?
Written by Rana DiOrio Illustrated by Chris Blair

What Does It Mean To Be Global?
Written by Rana DiOrio Illustrated by Chris Hill

Your Fantastic Elastic Brain: Stretch It, Shape It
Written by JoAnn Deak, Ph.D. Illustrated by Sarah Ackerley

The Owner's Manual For Driving Your Adolescent Brain
Written by JoAnn Deak, Ph.D. and Terrence Deak, Ph.D. Illustrated by Freya Harrison

Grown-ups, the World, and Me!
Written by Judith Lazar and Roger Pare Translated by Elisabeth Lore

A Bird on Water Street
Written by Elizabeth O. Dulemba

Fireflies: A Writer's Notebook
Written by Coleen Paratore

The Cow in Patrick O'Shanahan's Kitchen
Written by Diana Prichard Illustrated by Heather Devlin Knopf

Spaghetti is NOT a Finger Food
(and Other Life Lessons)
Written by Jodi Carmichael Illustrated by Sarah Ackerley

BIG
Written by Coleen Paratore Illustrated by Clare Fennell

Ripple's Effect
Written by Shawn Achor and Amy Blankson Illustrated by Cecilia Rebora

Snutt the Ift: A Small but Significant
Chapter in the Life of the Universe
Written and Illustrated by Helen Ward

Sofia's Dream
Written by Land Wilson Illustrated by Sue Cornelison

www.littlepicklepress.com